GREENSTREET

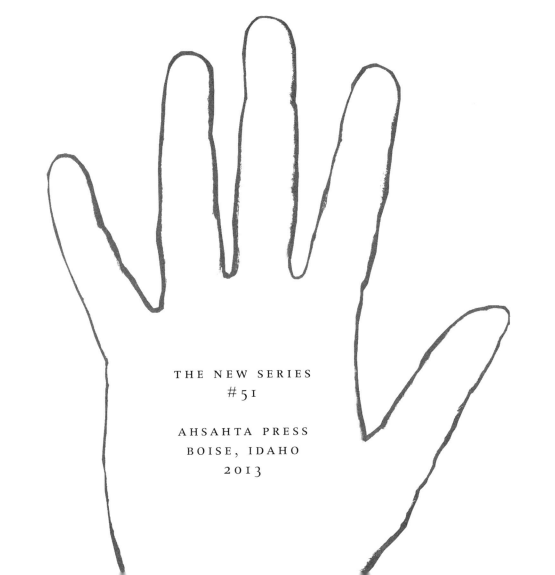

YOUNG TAMBLING

KATE GREENSTREET

Ahsahta Press
Boise State University, Boise, Idaho 83725-1525
ahsahtapress.org

©2013 Kate Greenstreet
Cover design by M & K Greenstreet
Book design by Kate Greenstreet and Janet Holmes
Artwork by Kate Greenstreet
Printed in Canada

First printing January 2013
ISBN 978-1-934103-35-7

Library of Congress Cataloging-in-Publication Data
Greenstreet, Kate.
Young Tambling / Kate Greenstreet.
p. cm.—(The new series ; 51)
ISBN 978-1-934103-35-7 (pbk. : alk. paper)—ISBN 1-934103-35-7 (pbk. : alk. paper)
I. Title.
PS3607.R4666Y68 2013
818'.603—DC23
2012029812

ACKNOWLEDGMENTS *Young Tambling* contains some work from five chapbooks: *Rushes* (above/ground press 2007), *This is why I hurt you* (Lame House Press 2008), *"but even now I am perhaps not speaking"* (Imprint Press 2010), *Called* (Delete Press 2011), and *our weakness no stranger* (Red Glass Books 2012). Many thanks to the editors of those presses and to the editors of Bonfire Press, Flash+Card Press, the Academy of American Poets' Poem-A-Day series, *Bird Fly Good*, *Black Warrior Review*, *Boston Review*, *Cannibal*, *Chicago Review*, *Colorado Review*, *Columbia Review*, *Court Green*, *Denver Quarterly*, *Dewclaw*, *Drunken Boat*, *Fascicle*, *Fence*, *GlitterPony*, *Guernica*, *Handsome*, *Harp & Altar*, *Headlamp*, *Hotel Amerika*, *InDigest*, *jubilat*, *Make*, *Martha's Vineyard Arts and Ideas*, *Ocho*, *Peep/Show*, *Phoebe*, *Ping Pong*, *Poor Claudia*, *Raleigh Quarterly*, *Saltgrass*, *Sink Review*, *Sugar House Review*, *The Offending Adam*, *the tiny*, *Vanitas*, *Volt*, and *Women's Studies Quarterly*, where parts of *Young Tambling* have appeared.

Big, big thanks to Janet Holmes.

NARRATIVE	1
ACT	31
MEMORY	65
FORBIDDEN	97
SUNG	127
WE	149

The narrative inhabits
its proper dark.

FRANK KERMODE

They say you're a headstrong girl. You run into the woods and pull a double rose. This is later thought to be symbolic. But today, you just pick the flower and he appears, as though called. If you were warned not to come here, he's the reason why. He pulls you down. Is it wrong? When it's done, according to the song, you turn "to ask your true love's name." But he's gone, and the woods grow dim.

The characters are introduced. A situation that begins to demand a set of changes. The ballad is named for him, although he is not the hero: Tam Lin, Tom Line, Tamlane, Young Tambling. There are many variations. Is he elven or human—is he trapped between worlds? He was enough in your world to leave you pregnant. A servant suggests an herb that will invite miscarriage. Traditional ballad narratives are episodic, relying on dialogue and action. Back to the woods, your father's woods, to pick the bitter herb and suddenly he's there again, saying: why do that when you could have the baby, and me, and a whole new life.

Seems like some people are born waiting for something—always listening, or looking, feeling toward the future. Other people—it just happens and they don't know what hit them.

Nearly half of the 305 ballads that Francis Child collected in the late 1800s are tales of romantic love and/or crimes of violence related to sex. Polly Stewart asks "what are the lessons women might learn from these ballads?" and concludes "that a man will take from a woman what he can and will punish her for being his victim; that a woman's needs are not a primary consideration either for her family or for men outside her family . . . that a woman's resources for protecting her interests are slim indeed." This ballad is an exception.

When they meet in the woods the second time, Young Tambling tells Margaret (in other versions, Janet, or Jennet) that he has been kidnapped by the Queen of Elfland and he describes in detail how he can be rescued. There are rules, which mainly involve holding on to him tightly, fearlessly, while he is turned into a lion, then a snake, a red-hot coal or bar of iron, and finally into a naked man, whom she must hide with her mantle.

For once, the hero is the girl, and her point of view and actions are the primary focus as the story unfolds. "It's so rare, even to this day, incidentally, that a woman drives the narrative of a drama." By the end, because he owes her his life, we might imagine that these two could embark on something like an equal partnership. Though that was probably impossible in the sixteenth century. It's a modern idea.

Sometime in the late twentieth century, I'm taking a new record from its sleeve. The singer is someone I've heard about and what I've heard intrigues me. This is her first album, just out and available only in the UK. As I set the needle down, looking at the surface of the vinyl, I notice the extra-wide, ten and a half minute track "Young Tambling." She will sing it unaccompanied. I will listen unaccompanied.

The narrative inhabits its
proper dark.

FRANK KERMODE

It was in the mountains.

She got hit by lightning, and wandered for a while.
Only one thing disappeared.

—Do you think of poetry as useful?

—Yes, it has been to me.

—Tell me some of the ways it has been useful to you personally.

—It makes me feel that being human is a good thing. Being human, and even just being the way I am . . . I'm not completely alone.

—So a use of poetry is to feel connected to other people?

—To feel human. And to feel that being human is . . . an okay thing.

—It makes you feel that being human is an okay thing because it allows a connection between you and others?

—I guess. I guess it makes me feel like we're all okay somehow. [starts to cry]

—How does poetry cause that feeling?

—I don't know.

I was outside and inside at the same time. We were all sitting at a table, in a way, but we were also out on the street and there was a dead deer in the street. I went over to it and sat down on the curb. The deer lifted himself then, his bloody head and all, into my lap. I didn't know what to do. He seemed to be talking to me, in a language I couldn't understand.

I didn't know if, because he was wounded, he might harm me—out of desperation. But I didn't want to push him away. He would put his head down in my lap, then lift it up—to look at me and speak. After a while I realized he wasn't really talking—it was a machine, inside him.

Who can be represented by art?

Who can be involved
in the making
of art?

A handful of people
were killed,
we heard.

Ten brothers sat for a portrait.
I was behind them
for so long.

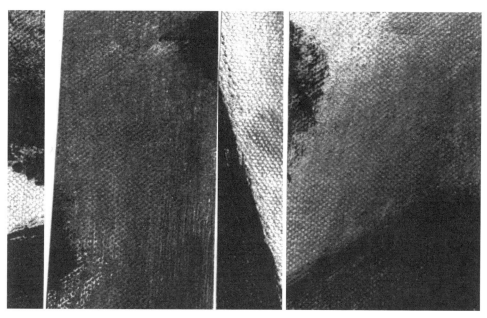

They want to bury you. Even while they're saying nice to meet you, they dump a little dirt onto your shoe.

A taped record of a trial was coming from inside him (I somehow knew). I thought it might be evidence. And I thought it might be important. Now, for the first time, I noticed he was cut in half.

Tell me what you most want to tell me. You're a twin, you have AIDS, your brother died? You were so close to your little one but—because of the divorce—or because of things you can't explain, she won't talk to you now.

How many people can you fit in your hand? Can you describe a color or a texture? Sunflowers, really? They can grow in the closet? Don't they need light—their throats?

Light from within. To light my candle for the feeling of "receive me."

Your clothes are dry now. (Talking to the gravestone.)
We call this pattern universal.

She knows her way, or she's just walking.
Her first day, she meets a friend.

The picture should be looked at with its case not fully
opened, preferably in private and by lamplight.

The deer had apparently been sawn in half, lengthwise, and there was a cloth, a black cloth stretched flat, where the back of his body would have been.

It was like the back of an old-fashioned radio or hunting trophy, that black cloth. Here he was in his halfness, that part done.

Do you have a question?

Some say it's the heart, some the brain.

You can't decide which of three people will live and who will die, but I can.

This story takes place everywhere.
The flying birds, the window, the sun
makes a hexagram. That golden light on the motel.

He'd lift up, he'd look at me. At those times, he would seem to be whole. And this talk, this recording, would emanate from him. He seemed to need me. Where can art be found?

I feel for the lamp and it's gone. Black is missing.
The red has a point but no lead.

They are not portraits if the word is taken.
We call this pattern unlived.

You look worried. Don't be. There were people before us, first-name basis. Chris, Eva, Joseph, Agnes, Joan.

Spend a hundred years, twenty years, forty years—highway, smokestacks, the long coats, the writing in reverse, then I forgot about it. Now I'm considering.

What sustains her? Begins with no.
She would open that narrowness.

The picture should be looked at. In the dream it's you and me and a lot of other people. We're performing a long and complicated vocal piece and I love you in the dream.

I think it lasts about . . . twenty minutes. Then they have to use the hack saws. To get it off. Can we recognize a pattern?

You seemed to need me but—when you put those big hooves in my lap? How can I recognize the real thing? Sometimes the tiniest breeze will set it off. People don't get over it. Women, never. This is the devil's work, this mirror.

I wondered if he would die in my arms. And if I would understand the evidence. And I wondered . . . what I'd do. If he didn't die. This went on for quite a while.

At one point, he seemed well again, he was kneeling, and he threw a blue blanket over our heads so he and I were in this tent of blanket and the light was very blue. We were looking at each other and I said, "I love you." And he laughed this sort of short laugh and said, "Spoken like a true Christian."

The night works by slowing. "I've always known" is a way to name it. He had these big sharp claws on his hooves, and sometimes he'd put one up on me. I understood it as the part of our mind where art comes from. And I hoped he wouldn't scratch me with them, because that would really hurt.

I am sending you a book that might be useful.
Red is the devil. Gold is God.

There's a place where we're walking down the road together.
A moment that can only be returned to in one way. Go with
great care.

It's logical to say that what I do
is an act of faith. It came to me.
And I worked it out.

WALKER EVANS

We didn't have another world to go to, but we had books. We had the library downtown. I think my best friend and I must have read every book in the young adult section by the time we were ten (that word "adult" attracted us), at least all the ones about girl detectives and romance and careers. We liked to sing on the swings, dance to records in the basement, talk about boys, act out dramatic scenes (birth, death). But I also needed to be alone. To think. My mother gave me the tiny room off the kitchen, where I could read and arrange things and listen to music on the radio. My father and my grandmother felt it was excessive for a child to have a room of her own (before this I was in the big room with my brothers), but my mother made it happen.

My room had a counter running the length of one wall—I loved this counter, the top was red linoleum. I used it mainly as a place to build small shrines. My father was constructing an archway into the living room (took about five years to finish) so there were often pieces of wood and plasterboard around. I might take a chunk of 2×4, cover it with a good white handkerchief, then set or stack things on it: to look at them. Rocks, dollhouse furniture, stuff I'd find on the sidewalk—or make, out of sticks and tin foil. This was almost an impulse toward sculpture, but I thought of my structures as altars, or shrines. I always had an urge to put things together that didn't belong with each other until they were arranged, by me, in just the right way.

We moved away from the city when I turned 15. My mother was 36. All the women on our new street were mothers. They must have been mostly in their early thirties, their kids were still small. It was a pretty nice street. My mother was so happy to be in a place with trees. There were giant cracks in the life—we take that for granted now because that's how the time is portrayed. But the women had their houses and their children, their marriages. Their husbands came into the dry cleaners where I worked after school.

When I think of them—Eleanor, Carolyn, Florence, Julie, Mary Ann—they seem trapped on that street. But on other streets, Barbara Guest was alive, Joan Mitchell was alive, Agnes Martin was alive.

I got the job in the cleaners soon after we moved. That's one of the places I learned about the kinds of things that happen to girls. Because you'd be there alone, most of the time. I learned a little bit about people. Mainly, I read. When it wasn't busy, you'd just sit there until someone walked in. So I read a lot, which was great since I always was trying to find more time to read.

The guys in back did the cleaning and pressing in the first part of the day. When I got there, I'd bag, staple the tickets to the plastic bags of clothes, and lift the clothes onto the conveyer. It could be heavy work for a person of my size, but I got stronger. The hardest thing about the job was how everybody came in all at once—Saturday morning, Friday night. That made me nervous, because people would be in a hurry and there'd be a long line. But I found I could do the job, and even like it. I did it for years, all through high school and, after that, full-time. I was supposed to go to college. I'd been accepted, but I didn't want to go. Not that I intended to stay in town forever. But at the cleaners, although I interacted with people, I didn't have to try to be one of them. It was different from school in that way.

In those years, I was especially attracted to books from the nineteenth century. I read a lot of stuff in translation. As a younger girl, I'd loved books in series—from there I went on to long books. I liked a large word-count. By this time, the friends I had weren't reading what I read. But the books were also my friends. There was a kind of fidelity involved. I didn't need to share them. I was faithful.

"She remains in the background, or, to say it better, elsewhere." The time I was living in while reading wasn't the time I occupied writing down N S for "no starch." Shifting between the world of my book and dealing with whoever walked through the door was immediate and natural. Like any double life.

Later on, I would read to relax. But back then, I didn't need relaxation. I needed to learn. And I needed to love. Not that I didn't love anyone—but I needed to love *more*. I read to encounter characters I could love deeply. In Russian novels and plays, people jumped up from the table and said things. And they weren't shocked if other people did—it was expected! I believed life took place in conversation. Or that it could. I wanted to somehow slip "through the barriers into the company of the Real Ones." I was just starting to paint, and I hoped to be an artist someday.

It's logical to say that what I do
is an act of faith. It came to me.
And I worked it out.

                    WALKER EVANS

"detuned"

Not dirt, but the dust of dirt. My whole life is here. I can show you, on the map.

If it was a wood, a deep ravine, or water . . .

"If you start talking, I'm leaving" and they both put on their coats.

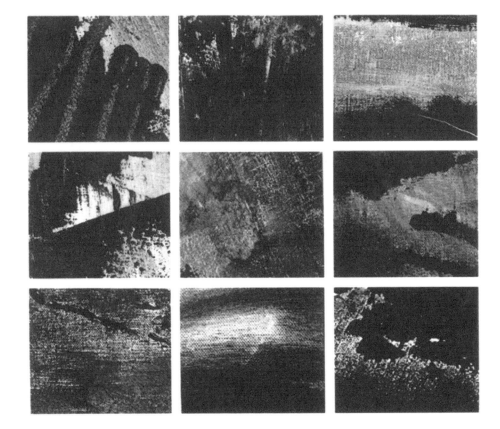

But what about fog?

What about
anonymity?

The men seemed strong but they've chosen

the wrong side. Instead of leaving,
he takes off his coat.
Countless hours in trance. He says
he can't breathe.

You are afraid
because

You are afraid that,
after all

PLATE I: STANDS AT HER HALF-DOOR
"Even the truth . . . sometimes I confuse this world with the other."

>The song recalls a day.
>Those who went west with little but a cross,
>the mother's good china.
>
>Those who came back?
>*How often I dreamed . . .*
>
>
>Obviously, things move
>or don't move.
>
>He comes early, sets out his tools.
>Ultramarine
>and black. Dark lake
>and black. Carmine. Ochre.

Picture of a family wearing the memory of a house.

Orange.
Orange-red, and black.
Violet,
gray-black. Gray-black
and black. Pale green.

Toward the plains.

We know a little bit about the driver.
The red kimono is wrong.

He had a brother, who died when they were young.
Who was older, and handsome.

I think everybody wants to hear
why it happened—what's on the other side
of that wall.

Animal to person, person to plant.
Who's not going to accept a call?

Mostly, we kind of liked each other.

I could remember the life
in the chair, the mirrors hung to misdirect misfortune.
The little one with the little flowers—
something something May . . .

Now they say Beethoven's hair was full of lead.

You can relax, enough
to see black. What you've lost? I believe
it has frozen the soap to the glass.

First we hear it. Trucks, helicopters.
The Battleship Potemkin. He's building the shape.

My white dress, my telescope.

Maybe I can think of another way to say this.
We were in a small rowboat.

And suddenly we saw a church.

PLATE 2: SETS THE BAG ON THE TABLE
"These stand for hope."

We shouldn't tell ourselves stories
about a better world

It's just a life
What you find around you

So many fish in those days

Here's my explanation of death: There is no water.

Opening the ardor: lightning.
Opening the door: belong.

Home was the place
How often I dreamed
        I was already in the west

Like any postman
with a thousand paintings in his attic

Home to the lamp

The desire to be a soldier.
It's like the desire to be a mother. Some parts are weak.

"A lamp in my work
might make you think of a police interrogation, but
it's also religious, like a candle."

Right before the funeral,
one of us slipped and broke his leg.

PLATE 3: CLUMPS OF EARTH, LIKE STARFISH ON A BEACH
"Why are all you boys alive?"

No ties, no great need.

But, as a life can be shaped by rumor, often there's a brother.

Who went away, who is told now: stay out of it.
This was the case that night. I knew the door he meant.

Help me get out of here. And we'll go back to being ourselves.

He turns off the music.

As if it were music
in the room.

I don't remember.
Who I was waiting for.

I think my parents should've spoken to each other more
openly, but it's hard to do.

People devote their lives—they start on a course . . .
Now that I'm here, I could be anyone.

I don't remember
what I was wearing.

I was always driving someone somewhere.

PLATE 4: THE ITEMS, ONE BY ONE, PLACED INTO THE CASE
"Whose sexy thing is this?"

    She's smart enough
    and she's been a servant.

    Crossing the field
    or frozen-over lake.

    Does she have money? to pay for that?

    All these soldier pictures are the same.

PLATE 5: NOT A STAR, A WINDOW
"To understand what happens with the shadow of a tree—"

it might have to do with how the earth is spinning.
Never wait for people to come back.

But all I care about is that we would speak.

Everything hurt. I was burning. It won't stay in the past.

PLATE 6: IT WAS A TIME OF VISIONS
"and what have you that you did not receive?"

She never doubts she can see what is hidden, lost.
Breath on the glass. Spent fuel.
Calls it the ghost.

In the beginning, I came to live.

Still in sight of the mirror,
the landscape
enters.

It's the one room I can't leave.

What else was happening that day,
or how did it get buried? Now he's a different boy.

Called, identified, drafted, named.
Cried out.
I thought, then, I would marry a soldier.

But I don't use the streets.

Meeting in a field? In real life, who knows.
Things that happen, things that don't happen.
Why a girl might wish to hear certain words.

The building is designed to make you look to heaven.

The ice?
A lake.

Two years after he disappeared, I woke, having dreamed of him.

Not a kind person.

Unfinished?
Held.
Like the rope that breaks.
Could be surprisingly decent
at times.
Interested in music.
Physically fearless.
Addict.

"I'd like to talk about loneliness. I don't believe it exists."

Tell me
the first truth
about it.

The exact reason
she kneels. Unbrittle,
unsharp.

I've felt like that—you understand? We had to go back.
To some town . . . or maybe a road . . .

I like her. I remember her.

I remember that—her running up the stairs.
Later, she dives into the leafy pool.
To forget.
The dream of art.
The dream of the body.

Is there another dream?

Not much has changed in the future.

Various colors
are not invented. People started teaching me Spanish.

Shapes
come to him. The life behind the life.
Ella es un cuarto para ellos.

PLATE 7: FOR SOME TIME HE HAD BEEN WORRIED
"The experience depends on the way in which a memory is retrieved."

It's still a story of two brothers.

I'm writing down what I think I heard.

Not at first. But now.

We got out to stretch. Just the guy selling boots.

Over in the corner of the lot. All sizes.

I hate to see people so happy.

One tree on the shady side, hiding birds.

I could never get too close to him physically. We hadn't taken any main roads.

That same day M. stuck his walking stick into the imprints left by horses' hoofs on the roadway — it had been raining the day before and they were full of water. "Like memory," he said.

NADEZHDA MANDELSTAM

I keep thinking of—what was her name? Terry. From San Clemente. She had pain and they "took a look" and it was all through her body. They gave her two months and she died in two months. That was it. She had kids. Something is definitely moving in there. It's like having a cat in there.

—What else?

Just people, different people. My mother. I just see her, you know? Things she wanted. I'm so tired. I was remembering my first communion. The main thing about it was the veil. The veil had this elastic aspect and two awful little bows that slid forward into my eyes when the elastic would creep. You couldn't push them out of your eyes because you had to keep your hands folded. I hated the whole thing of getting dressed up in this outfit. But I did like receiving communion. I always liked that. I didn't like leaving my seat. Walking up to the altar, you were sort of exposed. But I liked taking it onto my tongue.

—The wafer?

The Eucharist. The Host. We never called it "the wafer," that's for sure. I think Protestants might call it that. I mean, it *is* a tiny thin wafer made of bread. But for Catholics, it's not a symbol. For Catholics, that item is the body of Christ, no two ways about it.

—And you liked taking the body of Christ right into your mouth.

Within me! Within me, yes. I could go back to my seat and feel Jesus within me. And I would get really, really happy. Sometimes I would imagine dancing over the tops of the pews in my happiness. I remember that. Well, you know, it was a powerful idea.

I used to wonder if I had a call. That's something you're taught in Catholic school: certain people have a call to be a priest or a nun. I thought it might happen to me. I thought about being a nun, a lot. A different kind of nun than the ones I had. I would behave differently and have a different habit. The Sisters of Charity had these terrible habits. But some other nuns looked good.

I was a conscientious student, so I did okay in school, mostly. But around fifth grade, I started getting in trouble about my uniform. I liked to wear my belt *tight*, not wear the tie, open the top button of my shirt, and not wear the shoes. The belt was cloth—you were supposed to let it just hang on you, loose. But I wanted to have a figure. You know. I wanted to be like an older girl.

The shoes were a new addition that year. They were very round and heavy—and blue, like the uniforms, just to make it worse. I had my little red flats that I liked.

—Hat?

The hat! I forgot. I hated the hat, so I'd forget it then, too. Genuinely. When I arrived at school without it, I'd get yelled at. Obviously, I had to button my shirt and put the tie on. I would try to do that before I got on line. You had to get on line before you went in to the classroom. Then file in. I would put my hat on then, if I had it, but a lot of times I would've forgotten it, by accident.

Some of the older girls used to do the thing of folding the hat over. It was a kind of beanie with a bill. They'd fold it over—the cool girls—and pin it to their hair with a little bobby pin. They had this big gorgeous hair and they'd get it all just right and then they'd pin the half-a-hat on. I never got the knack. My hair wasn't big enough.

I was afraid to get in trouble, really, but sometimes, like if I walked home for lunch, I'd return wearing this certain sweater of my grandmother's with my uniform, no tie (I'd leave the tie home), and my red flats. The sweater was white and red—a patterned cardigan, like the ones that are back now. How could these improvements be worth the flak! I don't know, it was as if I couldn't help myself sometimes.

So yeah, I disliked school but church was good. I liked praying in church when I was young. You kneel down and lean your folded hands against the pew in front of you and rest, and talk to God. It was nice.

I think I could sleep now, if I closed my eyes.

That same day M. stuck his walking-stick into the imprints left by horses' hoofs on the roadway—it had been raining the day before and they were full of water. "Like memory," he said.

NADEZHDA MANDELSTAM

"future in the past"

Breaking things because I couldn't hold onto them.

Today,
like every day, what's missing?

What might be missing.

She dove from a high place,
broke her tooth. On the breath, calls it back.

See what the room sees—hand
and foot—your face

on that small screen.

People often ask me why my photographs are torn.
The purpose would be

to learn. To represent a life.

"curtain wall"

The wood belongs to the father.

I have the feeling that he set to work.
It took him years. What is experimental?

No blood,
just cooking. Same as you.

I miss the sun. The sound
of their voices.

Which has been covered with a white cloth.

My shadow, his shadow, his
hand's shadow.

"You got a visitor, baby."

He was alone in that house.
There was a door, a social context.

I often wanted to enter his home.
But even now I am perhaps not speaking.

Knocked
into the pink hourglass.

The close and far,
the empty pool, the columns.

That's how I feel when I'm being her.

I shook hands with the men.

I'm disappearing.
Something
in me
is disappearing.

So. Is that a yes?

Some of us have taken off our wigs.
The immense, the colossal weight
of our hope. Sex is part of it.
Do you think I'm pretty?

"she ventures in"

I change the focus of my eyes,
then I can see.

It's come over him. Not from afar.
That's him grown—what does he hear?

From the room of his time

and the room
of his room   "this is evil"

without shadow
a thing can be seen

as it is, he said

I was looking for a way to look
at the world   "it was my need to feel"

there is a history in me
he said   "these two pictures are the same

picture"   when it was done

thinking herself
alone, she began to sing

We found her in the churchyard, writing on herself.
Just a sentence, but it had a title: "arms."

Pulls out the plants.

Threw up a steel fence.

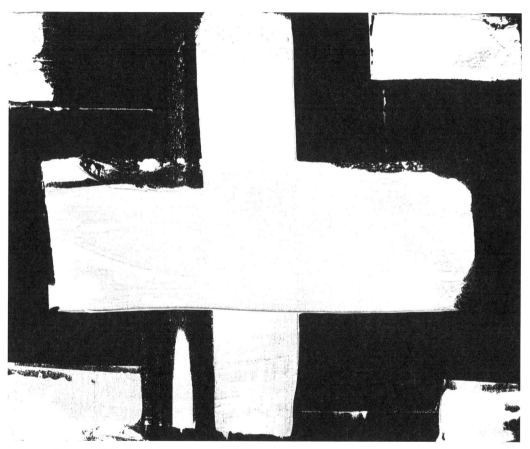

See, I'd still be there but my organs would be gone. My eyes. How power works. Power over.

"a body being outlined"

Pink among the statues. Dark
around the edges, like a tunnel.
Look at all this junk.

"These paintings
were made with blood."
He claimed he wrote it in one night.

Deplore.
Apace.
When you're with the puppet.

I chose the better looking habit.

Very clean and white. Very white.
Before the first word is spoken.

"I did it. Did you see me?"

"he did not rave"

Lies right down, we take our shoes off.
Ghost as verb.

"I cannot move the phantom."

"unshot"

Not a paper frontier. The world
reflected in the place you are,

something you need to see that you cannot see directly.
Eyes passed over, eyes
hold the imprint. And so the stream breaks apart.

I remember water, the mountain, three months.
These girls remind me of real girls.

I know the room that was my father's room.
Guided to the stairs, the mountain.

Remember Tanya? She was a mean girl.
When you leave your house, you step outside.

The stream erupts into a wide and endless river.
Often it was the case that the man who asked the question
did not recognize the answer.

"but as I am not I shall turn"

Let me sing it for you.
Something about "from now on."

We know her face. She's not afraid to smile that way.

Photogenic
is only the beginning.

Still resembles my idea of what a friend is.

Lost.
Knocked.

I hope you didn't blame me much.

"open voicings"

A shadow broke the light beneath the door.
You're leaving us so soon? It's a song about betrayal.

Did you ever see a bunny fly? What is abstraction?
Some things we didn't know.

It's a song about a girl who listens.
I explained a part to you.

She's been a child. She has a child's love.

Later, when we were walking, I could see that she was spelling, in her mind, the words that we were saying, and from time to time she stopped to write one down, if the letters were right.

"they can get lost, they burn"

He really doesn't like it when I'm too polite. But he also sometimes doesn't like it if I'm not polite enough.

Page ten, the word "absconded." Underlined. And put into parentheses. So—when they sit down and say "Well, I don't even know why I'm here," don't they mean "Can't you help me?"

"It rained, all the day appointed" (page 24). Given the water, the windows in the train, the darker humors—

but—a special way of
[sigh]
a special person . . .

It is not yet May, as a reason why not. Your presence dispels lies, as a reason why not. Page ten, handwritten in pen across the top: "run away secretly and hide."

"and everywhere I felt alone"

> He's tean her by the milk-white hand,
> And by the grass-green sleeve,
> And laid her lo at the foot of the tree,
> At her he askt no leave.   39[K]

I knew he was my enemy.

That's all I likened to. I heard the clap.
When you pick it up, this hunting gun . . .

I heard the clap and thought it was over.
Remember how the dresses dragged
on the ground between us?

—So what happened then?

That was the summer I turned 19.

—Take a long time?

Suddenly a storm came up. We went into the water
anyway.

Then a clap. Maybe
the report of a gun.
Someone's best friend went down.

—So how'd it work out?

That summer went by.
I remember the thunder. No one knew where we were.

—Take a long time?

There was a moment. He seemed to be
running away . . .

Once I was jumping on the bed in happiness and hit my
head on the ceiling. That marked the end.

P̶C̶O̶O̶U̶R̶E̶S̶ C̶O̶M̶E̶ B̶A̶C̶K̶ T̶O̶ M̶E̶ start
no N no D no L no G no H hurt no F art curate cue
petite   cruel pot
P̶I̶C̶T̶U̶R̶E̶S̶ C̶O̶M̶E̶ B̶A̶C̶K̶ T̶O̶ M̶E̶ cruet sax

patter bark   spatter   matter   base spear   Combat par
batter Mars   crate beam pour setter captor   Summer bump   par
        sect   mark crisp   crook   smote
rest crumpet left crimes act   boast   took peck   smoke
respir(e?) caper comb pure   barter care pact lost NoL   come
         mare leap maker   accuse cob   sack   puce
bat   tomb   master rapt cope STAR combat NoL oak rise
tic-tock mere take care   root case rebuke books tome Bee Crea
       coop aim   pock
meet   Kris Rick rebuke beer morter but   rate puke plectr crib
       Booker   pack   soot
picked Mac Skip steam mature past troops rape   fact
rock   cure   pork   malm? Pick truck   pubic mule
       Sam Piet steak NoL   self   tape   cork taper
mock   Tom bruh cop   crater ?   broom   toc(K) crank rope
seat   Kate Mia cure cameo   butt   time(s)   tank spea
keep   Pat Irq   beat cookies Creep best Rescue   butter bank spoke
crest matt   took NoL   muller pest pocket rook brook   broke
script Tim mose berate bear   sent blame NoL soot apt   puce
best   no scent bum   perk suck rib mask bare
or   Sue bitter beak crop   muti   races muck ape east stave
beat   Kim   crock at must sent   port sub kite coast post
trick Lari Bea talk   paste pram poker club ace   screa
coo   Rob Reba accept NoL rat   tram   sire
sick   babe ears   tramp take tub suck   tore
kept   Peter Casper pet pear cock stoop moot cub simmer
treat Mike Beth mores mate poems mist muff   cat court tears
reek   Tom   set crumbs cramp peruse at pace pie
eat   mae BOO bore comma cost stamp cadmium Crust sour sure course Stuck
seek   mark   met coma   most Tacoma put   buck   rice rumor
escort   poster   smear   stop   mambo mate
peek   Kurt tore tubes   post Tibet ur spice
be   Maurice taupe tuba mire Paris out spice make meat cots
       Mom mira Corl breast   Peru cook potato   rake
me   Pam Bruce   brim   poke mecca meek soap   toe brakes
sake   use   saucer
see   storm   sop   coke trust sear bake soup cake   break
              mop memo   cocoa Cork seer cream mace pace suit tumor
       spice tort sum   Cuba mised pours braces port tea cup
pout   tomato mor mope some soak Europe robe

cam

I don't make them stop.
~~bit~~ pose (backwards?)
~~bit~~   mob   probate sat   coupe
ube   super rebate spite
~~ce~~   superb   map   ~~market~~
ice
ste   ~~_____~~   ~~_____~~ slap   better
~~_____~~ ~~_____~~ market clap   ~~_____~~
scab
~~_____~~ cup   burp
          ramp tote rob
ester BIKE tree(s) sparmouse traces
oors   spore bar cat   casket
poor toot
cure   seem tart tame ~~_____~~
trace rite
skate coot seam torte same ~~_____~~
       raise scare ~~_____~~ mistake
scrike ease packet tip   mistook
       tease
tacit risk ~~brink~~   cars mister
       cite ~~sink~~   UPRISE ramore
mast   bracket crabs
mote raise escape compute porous
           racket   cram
rooms   bite scar crap ~~plum~~
pairs/rise strike   ~~_____~~
         cur   lute case
spokes   cape lout east robust
trip rack cape lout part
          mime loot stark meteor
                      sort
spit rose Arctic   sputter
totem mums pit miter crease
spook
risotto   cart meter bottom spree
teapot   carp   top   bucket
            tarp
member   skirt   boat   probe
     rump pant   boot
damp coat
tot roast panto   tapo brick

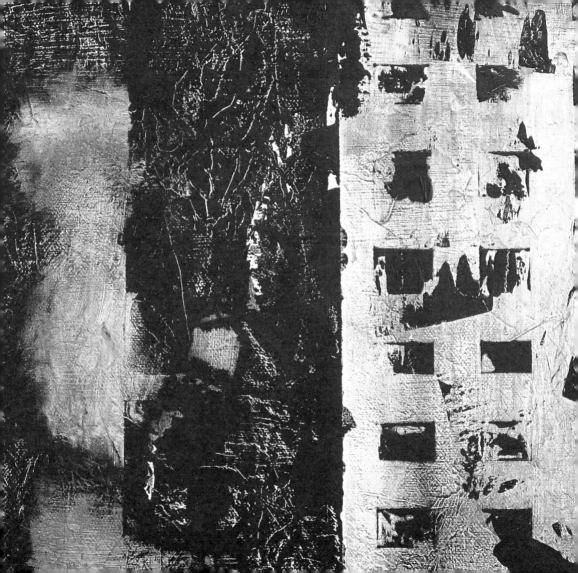

Perhaps we may awake one day,
alone or together. This we are
forbidden to know...

MAX BECKMANN

I was sitting on the porch, late, sometime after midnight. "Famous Blue Raincoat" playing in the kitchen, just loud enough to reach me through the screen. I heard a vehicle pull into the gravel, slow. No idea who it could be. He came toward me. The surprising absence of fear. I recognized him then—a friend of my brother's, from before. Didn't know him well. He had some records under his arm. We talked for a while about music. I had been away a few years.

Ice but no water, smoke but no fire. Air but no land, no earth. No ground, no dirt, no soil. No G, no H, no N, no L. Lots of people were talented. I knew them all. They liked the right music. A lot of people have talent, it's not enough. No F. No D. Of suicides, only 15% leave a note. The ones I knew: 0%. Hanged, hanged, OD'd, knife in the heart. Burned—

can't call it suicide. He walked out of the burning house and sat down on the curb. He was talking to himself when the firetrucks pulled up. Charred from head to foot. Art as we knew it (he said) was just designed to get us through our twenties. After that, you're on your own.

Voicing is working on the hammers themselves. He tried to come back and be who he was before. There was no picture. And he was saying that this very good friend of his had died. His face would be all red when he got off and he then he would make tea. He always fixed it then just the way I liked, and brought it in and spilled a little. Can't call it grief, it's not like a field you lay down in to drown—it's just some blades. Blades of the wrong kind of grass. Witchgrass, twitch grass, panic grass.

I notice things missing all the time. Themes. Language, and themes. They beat her to death because she loved the wrong person. And you can still find that in the news today. "A woman was enjoying a night out." I had a suit like that once. White. With a sheer black blouse. What should she have done? I was taught that God chooses you. I knew he wasn't chasing me around the basement because he loved me.

The refrain broke the sequence. "I could still see you naked sometimes?" What is that story of Camus', where the woman climbs a hill and offers herself to the night? Is there such a story? This is almost my story.

I loved the way he showed me his upholstery. One cut, against the grain. Don't ask me did it really happen, you know it did. One night we each told the saddest word. You said *no*, she said *please*, I said *wait*.

—You said you wouldn't hurt me.
—I lied.

Perhaps we may awake one day,
alone or together. This we are
forbidden to know.

                                      MAX BECKMANN

She took the car? Maybe. Men go to sea.

It comes into every serious and
beautiful life, she said.
A moment

when the person is listening, trying to bring in a signal.

I'd think I heard it, night after night,
but it was never there
on the tapes.

Doleful is the word that keeps coming to mind.

The family
is sleeping. A rock
or believed to be a rock

or ball of something, fallen from the sky.

What's allowed? Really.
What's allowed now?

He says
he understands me. It's like a game.

Why did he have a red hammer? That's a good question.

I remember we were crossing a desert.
I remember that no one could say
what they felt.

I thought he was different

and better
than everyone else.
I felt he could see me. Everything was there to teach us.

"locating faraway objects"

This is a ruby: an area of memory
set aside. (Rides a boy's bike. A detail.)

When you watch the rushes a second time,
the story of her experience,
the lost coat, shots fired at the sky—

Forsworn. Maybe a second too green.

Takes a picture of the coffee cup, his black shoes
on the rug. He says: "I'm working these two days."
Sends the photos from his phone.

I make the translation again.

Forsake.
For what the future may hold.

A slight adjustment toward plain darkness.
Lay thus.

It must have been great at first. The gravel lane,
the white phone, the cakes. That lampshade,
we had. Absolutely exact.

A family was standing in a high place.
Down in the street, a car beeped
and then they all waved. You see what it becomes.

He was a boy once.
He remembers
his father. And all the men.

He rebuilds the maze, he'll bring his son here.

Why do you laugh? are you afraid?

Will you sit here 'til I fall asleep?

She has her habit in the suitcase.
Even a stone can disappear.
And now this. This is really hard.
Yes. Or "be a man."
Imagine how strong he'd need to be.

Please don't tell me more about the future.

As you've heard
it has started
to
snow
again
snow
chains
on the mountain
roads
chains
are needed
What light!
He beats her.
And everybody knows.

Here's the house, still white.

Arms
Sight
Absence

The life I'd have. Giant apples?
or the first red leaves? What else did he like?
Let's go under those trees.

She looks after them
with concern. How long? Considering the ties
of that year. The knots. Was it just a sex thing?

We were looking for a street.

There had been
some kind of earthquake.
And I remember this part very clearly—

Something so familiar, not from now
but—it's like dating a statue. I mean,
500 BC . . . 600 BC . . . dating it.

There were no men. I don't know why.
War.
Or just the time of day. Let me hear his name again.

I looked it up, but it wasn't there. I got
"Do I have to use a condom?" and
"Your camera doesn't matter."

Promise.
Swear not to.

The shelves are empty. Everyone's
lifetime.

I thought you didn't believe in sin.
Statue burns down, we make another statue.
There's a special name for
all of us are having the same dream.

Woke up screaming? Woke me up screaming.

I have a translation for you.

A dark corner, lit.

He's been off, fighting. Now he's back.
He tries to stay awake.

His method of curing his illness is to search for sounds.
Black baby, black baby—is it poison?

Did you hide? We put you in a car.
We put you in a car and drove as fast as we could.

Darkness came down, the way it does in winter.
It was snowing in the cutting room.

I can still remember the day you were born.
The cloth. Just the grain itself.

Light by six.
Like everyone, she's simple.

I understand her crazy trust.
But how can these tricks work?

Parks
at night

are always dangerous.
And our will. Free will.

She cuts herself. I never got close
to that.

The dog
has seen it all.

A piece of thinking.
And this is where she hears herself.

I lay on stones
and, next to me, the others.

They did not love me.
Is it a sin to love?

"quietly uneasy," she lets him in.

"As if you wanted to obliterate yourself."

As if realism = truthfulness.

But I'm moved by it: the shoes, the decision.

You told me I'd be lost.

Poor, or whatever comes first.

restore / resist
answer / count
what I'd give

He's afraid
the baby will be born like him, but the baby is fine.

On the legend, must the blue be the sea?
It's a story about this.

Fill in the blank: People are always _____.

Missing.
One way or another.

These are the woods where he grew up.

It's dark.
It's very quiet.

The dark pond.
Which is more filmic?

A photographic memory or amnesia?

He has an open place.

Safe
is an interpretation. Folds it like a flag.

Is all of the shame you feel
your fault?

The neighbors
are screaming again.
It's just a reaction to being invisible.

You know, they have pictures of the brain.
And the connections
are different.

Take off your coat.
It's wet. To save a drowning lamb?
I knew some crazy girls in my time.

I knew so many wild girls.

First thing that comes to mind
about who you were.

Sleeping on the floor
with the dog. I don't know. I just didn't know
what I was doing. I didn't know what I *could* do.

That night? we probably had tea.

He spent a long time talking about
how the shot was made.

It sounds like a riddle, but it is
no riddle . . . Song gives us the
experience we live only after
having sung the song.

DAN BEACHY-QUICK

"And of course we have it now, the sense of an ending."

We come upon the unexpected news of your death. It's a work day. Maybe all this sweating does some good?

St. Sebastian, top of head not rendered: that charcoal portrait you sat for on a rainy afternoon. The main thing is your idea (you said) of who you are. Then the rearrangement of the furniture, everyone in black. Though isn't there always someone in a dark color not black, because they don't have black. Or maybe, for once, I wanted to express myself.

A ballad tells a story. Sometimes, now, I think you're really in Brazil. Or Colorado. Free to start a different life, take up a different instrument.

The only man who thought no evil didn't live to write his introduction, so we can't know why he made certain choices. The request was incomplete. Incorrect, or impossible. Saying that you're friends, even feeling that you're friends, but not really *being* friends won't work out. You can't have a secret life, secret from your partner, and expect that to work. But everybody has their own thoughts. And what about that music? That music from upstairs.

Similarities: both are suffering, both are unreliable. Both are magical beings, hybrids. Each becomes immediately and inappropriately intimate. They are both in danger, and dangerous, in the wrong place. Try being me. Seems like every other day, somebody asks me what I am.

Drove down to the store for milk. Made conversation with Doris, drove home, under five minutes. Opened the car door and fell face first into the driveway. "Fuck," I heard myself say. "I must be higher than I thought."

Every week had a number, but sometimes a year was just a sentence. We took a walk and I sang a song for her. Not something I would normally do. "The Twa Brithers" is Child Ballad 49, there are many variants. Two brothers are wrestling when a blade that one of them is carrying mortally wounds the other. Occasionally, one of them stabs the other on purpose. What that song means to me: I let him go into the field with the gun. I didn't know what would happen and I didn't try to stop him. Why did so many women sing this ballad, and why did the few men who sang it only sing part?

"Ballads condense and focus areas of emotion and social pain, yet they are rather uncomplaining." I'm gonna say it amounted to this: it was raining. She had four kids already. I don't know—did they have kids together then, too? And they were doing music, living that life. She seems to have so much enjoyment in the music. The way she looks over at him. More than he looks at her. We were crossing . . . which war was it? Then he was born again. Wanted to give away the little they had, disappeared before a gig in Wisconsin. Just a marionette or—what do they call it?—a dummy. Back in the suitcase. You're the brother? I see her problem and I can't solve it. I don't have to write it down. I remember.

It sounds like a riddle, but it is
no riddle . . . song gives us the
experience we live only after
having sung the song.

DAN BEACHY-QUICK

The innocent? They're only there to distract you.
(Recalls an infidelity.)

As if the music is outside and, inside the room,
they can't hear it.

Language,
including nudity.
Signs hidden behind other signs.

Is it dialogue?
Is it description?

I like the distortions and haloes, etc.
I like the family pictures, but just to say goodbye.

He stands beside the body of the man he couldn't help.
For a moment they're alone.

It's such a long day
or
what a long day it's turning into.

She brings him some medicine.
When she starts to beg, he crumbles. Like dry soil. Even as he turns cold and hard, he's crumbling. Nothing holds. Nothing will transmit.

Now he'll be cruel. That's the human touch.

Is he going to take that medicine with him when he leaves?
At the doorway, he hesitates, asks: will she come with him. And she does! The medicine is left behind.

What will their days be like? Next week. Will they start a little business? Move somewhere else, get jobs, have savings?

The woman who asked to sit alone sits with us, instead.
I think the other man wants her, the one she doesn't love.
Does she only have two choices?

She prays. If only God would be a sport.

Sometimes she thinks that there's a fire.
One explanation is she's trying to escape the fire.

"suddenly as night"

With the wind came water, a door
"honest, and therefore
unmanageable."

When a gap opens,
he thinks it comes to him from God.

Well, you've gotta have your cookies, I know.
You gotta have your cookies
and your gun.

Meanwhile, I'm in the middle of writing my poem
about the city. Talking to the drapes. 100 bricks a day.

The pattern
is present in the room. More water!
May I not move you?

~~blame~~ no L   ~~talk~~ no L   ~~lock~~ no L

Because rain has been falling.
Because I always sing when I'm alone.

This type of chorus is called
a burden
because it was once submerged.
All our habitats
underwater:
Printing
Firearms
Medicine
Money
To put a spell on someone
or to break a spell.

Ever think your luck was really changing?

He should be able to save himself but the knife goes deep

into his left shoulder. I notice that I can feel it, though I'm just watching.

slow down

Because I like to sing a hard song.

Every day I rewrite the same poem. Now the town is gone, the girls are gone, "stay with me" is gone.

Over the buildings is like over the the water. If he makes all the stops, he'll never get out.

slow down
you have to feel it

you have to let yourself
stop

stop touching it

"bad ring"

The house where we last all lived together?
I'd never find that road now.
Four twelve? Four thirteen?

Each tree I loved
felled,
uprooted, long since. Most motives are mixed.

—And you're well from it? your history?

All that consoles me is my genius.

—But do you feel yourself to belong . . . to a certain period? A span of years, a decade?

When I see my brother. When I haven't seen him for a long time.

I asked him to bring me a newspaper from town.
Of course she was there too.

What is that song? There's a part that sounds like
"sentient beings." To condense—to fall
from the air.

You can't help thinking what you're looking for exists.
Blowing through the branches of the trees.

The smoke of our past, basket after basket. Tell me,
is it all forest around here?
Let me go on learning.

Trying keys. Tell me if it's good, just yes or no.

"I'm not an actor" and that day he quits his job.

I read him some poems while he chops onions; he goes up to write. I cook and drink, listen to whatever I'm listening to lately. Eyes of wood. Baby represents acting. Picture of a picture of a tree. Baby is so happy naked. The neighbor drives her to the store. Tension more than fear. The ice has some significance I forget. Broken glass? I'm a lucky person, but I never thought I was immune. Then we start to run.

"remove from me my heart of stone"

Just that fast, the light had shifted.
He began to speak. Think about how you want to live.

Basically, I'm talking about all those pictures.

Every wheel,
every mill.

Describes a different kind of work.

Ten thousand died, six thousand came to listen.
They're interested in violence. Imagine how much

you'd want to hear something else.

Use these words: the night so cold and no one on the road. Pull for a minute on a locked door.

"as if my name had been erased"

A memory of objects. Reimagined.

A completely new kind
of seeing. All gradations of light.

Trees huge at their base, like houses.
Thousands of miles.

From the roof,
the street. The windows black and lit.

Those slow connections we talked about.

Maybe you'd remember it all your life.

It's long but interesting,
the way that men and women are perceived.
If you need help, can I touch it?

Dear, I am the above-named person.
Move through space

with a place to return to: home.

Just as love is an enormous field,
many parts of it have to be imagined
by everyone.

Everything we dont understand
is explained
in Art.

                              AMIRI BARAKA

a) When I realized you weren't wise, I looked harder for God. Said he had a long gray beard, like ZZ Top. Said he's probably worth a hundred million. Said he was walking down the street with a wrench in his hand.

b) "Where do you go to be you?"

c) I always liked spending time alone. I thought painting might be something I could do. I liked the tools—the brushes, the trowels—the physicality of drawing, stretching canvases. I liked going around in clothes that were covered with paint.

d) My grandmother would say, "Another painting! Couldn't you get rid of some of these before you start doing more? The hall is loaded with them."

e) How does an addiction differ from a call?

f) In the museum, I look for a long time at a piece of art—it would be called minimalist—and I wonder about the day, the room, the light—what was the temperature as it was being made? My affection for the work is partly based on imagining the making, my empathy for the maker. Is empathy the word when you feel another's joy?

g) "Give it to me or strike me dead." There's nothing to do but feel the disappointment and see where it guides me.

h) "Some people, they start with the bugs—y'know, when they're kids? Always lookin' at the bugs and wantin' to know the different *names* of the bugs. Kids like that grow up, nobody's surprised if they're a scientist of some kind. But it could mean other things."

i) Some people decide to stop talking and pray instead. Like the trees are cleaning the air, they're praying for the world. Does that help? I have no idea. I doubt it, but we don't know what would happen if all the people praying for the world were to suddenly stop.

j) This has that sanded surface I used to do. Feel it. I'd put the paint on, then sand it off, partially—that's how I made them. Like making a charcoal drawing using mostly an eraser.

k) *You lack sufficient mobility, strength or dexterity. Reach upward, sideways, downward, grasp and push, pull, turn, shove, or otherwise open these mechanisms.*

l) He wrote a letter, and we're bringing what he asked for. Blue towels for curtains. Nylon underwear (dries overnight on the bars). He cares how things look.

m) When I look at my old work, I tend to see the problem I was having and how I tried to solve it. I see the weak place.

n) "Follow the painting all the way. Be in it; forced along with it, you will change. That's art."

o) —There's no such thing as drive without need. You've got to have something to prove. Or the feeling "this is not enough."

   —Is that why in paradise there is no art?

   —Yes.

p) To do what he did, he needed his instability. "You needed every part of yourself."

q) He had a job at a place where he was also living, but he couldn't practice there. So he'd drive into the woods to play. Banjo, fiddle, guitar—he was learning everything at once, by listening. He said we all have some kind of musical ability because we're made of tones.

r) I met a woman, a printmaker, after I'd been painting a few years. She told me she knew she'd never be a great artist or discover anything, she just liked making prints. That seemed sad to me then.

s) Where does art belong? What's it for? After you do it, where should it go?

t) I sure like my new pencil, which is transparent, mechanical, and aqua blue.

u) I need to *do* something with the stuff I'm ingesting, just being alive in the world. To use it, to see it, to place it in relationship to something else. I have to do that to keep going, and it's what I can do. It's what I'm fit for.

v) "The process is: you got a buncha shit laying around. Shit that's broken."

w) —The way you do art sounds like a kind of filtration system. Or dry cleaning! But instead of returning the clothes cleaned and pressed, you'd offer some other clothes instead.

—Or a pan of rocks, more like it. If you can live without the clothes and want the rocks, you've come to the right place. If you need those same clothes back, try the cleaners across the highway.

x) So many moments go unrepresented. You might be sitting on the toilet and hear yourself say "Joan Fontaine" in a low voice. His question: how do you live? A traditional description is "leaping" and "lingering." The small streets. The way the miles collect.

y) You're following a sound—it leads you off the road you were trying to stay on, and then, once you're good and lost, the sound goes quiet. I think that always happens! Then you have three choices.

z) He asked me to describe my relationship to despair. "Sisterly," I said.

Everything we dont understand
is explained
in Art.

AMIRI BARAKA

When I look at my old work — and really when I look at my newer work too — I see the problem I was having & how I tried to solve it. I see the weak place.

---

not autobiography but ABOUT biography

Dear reader, in case you want to know a little more—for instance, about page **3** In her essay "Tam Lin, Fair Janet, and the Sexual Revolution," Martha P. Hixton notes that three motifs listed in Seth Thompson's *Motif Index of Folk Literature* are present in the ballad "Tam Lin," the first being "Girl summons fairy lover by plucking flowers." Citing Barre Toelken, she states that plucking a rose is a basic metaphorical image for sexual activity in ballads, and points out that Janet/Margaret calls Tam Lin by plucking a rose (or two or three) in every variant. "Janet has power over Tam Lin in that, seemingly at least, he cannot appear until she summons him and this summons (picking the roses) is one he must obey." Hixton's essay is in *Marvels & Tales* (Wayne State University Press, 2004), 67–92. // In most variants, Margaret/Janet is warned not to go into these woods because of the presence of Tam Lin. But in the Anne Briggs version, there is no warning. **4** Polly Stewart, "Wishful Willful Wily Women: Lessons for Female Success in the Child Ballads." *Feminist Messages: Coding in Women's Folk Culture*, ed. Joan Newlon Radner (University of Illinois Press, 1993), 54–73. // Tam is a nickname form of the ancient Biblical and Hebrew name Thomas meaning "the twin." **5** "It's so rare . . . " Helen Mirren, in a radio interview. // According to Francis Child, the ballad "Tam Lin" dates back to at least 1549. He included 14 variants in *The English and Scottish Popular Ballads*, published in ten volumes between 1882 and

1898. // The ballad "Young Tambling" appeared on *Anne Briggs* (Topic Records, 1971). It can be found now on *Anne Briggs: A Collection,* a 22-song CD released by Topic in 1999. The songs are available on iTunes but the booklet that comes with the CD contains a 26-page essay by Colin Harper that tells more about the reclusive singer than you're likely to find anywhere else. **7** "That all narratives are essentially dark, despite the momentary radiance that attends divination, is a doctrine that would not have surprised pre-scientific interpreters . . . Even now, when so many theories of interpretation dispense in one way or another with the author, or allow him only a part analogous to that of the dummy hand at bridge, the position is not much altered; the narrative inhabits its proper dark, in which the interpreter traces its lineaments as best he can." Reprinted by permission of the publisher from *The Genesis of Secrecy: On the Interpretation of Narrative* by Frank Kermode, p. 45, Cambridge, Mass.: Harvard University Press, Copyright © 1979 by the President and Fellows of Harvard College. **14** Antony Gormley asks "Who can be represented by art? Who can be involved in the making of art? Where can art be found?" in Finn McAlinden's 2005 film *Broken Column*. **34** My mother was sitting up in bed. I was sitting on the edge of her bed. "I think I've formed my life around a wrong idea," she said. "What idea?" "That my life is a story someone else is watching." **36** "She remains . . ." Etel Adnan, *Of Cit-*

ies & Women (The Post-Apollo Press, 1993), 89. **37** "It is the Hand alone which has contrived to slip me through the barriers into the company of the Real Ones as Pursewarden used to say." Lawrence Durrell, *Clea* (Penguin Books, 1988), 278. **39** Leslie Katz, "Interview with Walker Evans," *Art in America* 59 (March–April 1971). **51** "A lamp in my work . . ." Christian Boltanski, quoted in *Photography Speaks*, ed. Brooks Johnson (Aperture Foundation, 2004), 302. **56** "For who makes you to differ with another? and what have you that you did not receive?" 1 Corinthians 4:7 **63** She is a room to them. **64** They tell a story of two brothers. One stays here on earth, it's called "missing time." **73** Nadezhda Mandelstam, *Hope Against Hope: A Memoir*, translated from the Russian by Max Hayward (Modern Library Paperback Edition), 197. English Translation © 1970 by Atheneum Publishers. **77** The curtain, a feature common to most medieval castles, was a set of walls that surrounded and protected the interior of the castle. **78** "But even now I am perhaps not speaking from myself: but from some character in whose soul I now live." John Keats to Richard Woodhouse, *The Letters of John Keats* (Kessinger Publishing, LLC, 2004), 211. **92** Child arranged his collection by assigning each ballad a number and then giving each variant a letter. 39[K] is the eleventh variant of the ballad "Tam Lin." **100** Beaten to death by her family because she loves the wrong man: "Mill o' Tifty's Annie" (Child

233: "Andrew Lammie"). **103** Max Beckmann, *On My Painting* (Hanuman Books, 1988), 73. **119** 8 July 2012: Received the final proof of *Young Tambling.* Later, packing to move, taking books off the shelves, I opened Paul Celan's *Collected Prose* (translated by Rosmarie Waldrop). Immediately noticed, embedded in two long sentences, the words that turned into lines three, four, and five. Some years ago, I'd tried to create a giant erasure from a stack of randomly photocopied passages, taken mostly from Swedish detective novels. Forgot there was a page of Celan's prose thrown in (I wouldn't typically use a poet's words in that kind of experiment). Long after abandoning the project ("my poem about the city"), I went through the drafts and felt attracted only to three phrases. Now I realize they all came from the same place. 9 July: Inserted this one last note. **129** Frank Kermode, *The Sense of an Ending: Studies in the Theory of Fiction* (Oxford University Press, 2000), 98. // William James called Francis Child "the only man I ever knew who thought no evil." Scott Alarik, "Child's Garden of Verses," *Sing Out!* (Volume 46 #4). **130** Thinking about similarities between the kidnapped Young Tambling and the deer who first appears on page 12. **131** About "The Twa Brithers," Lynn Wollstadt asks: "Why did so many women sing this ballad, and why did the few men not sing all of it?" in her essay "Reading Gender in the Ballads Scottish Women Sang." *Western Folklore*, Vol. 61, No. 3/4 (Autumn, 2002), 310. // "Ballads condense . . ." Rachel Blau DuPlessis, quoted on Ron Silliman's blog, January 10, 2005. **133** Epigraph by Dan Beachy-Quick, from *Wonderful Investigations: Essays, Meditations, Tales* (Minneapolis: Milkweed Editions, 2012). Copyright © 2012 by Dan Beachy-Quick. Reprinted with permission from Milkweed Editions. **135** "Signs hidden behind other signs." Jem Cohen in his 1996 film *Lost Book Found*. **138** "honest, and therefore unmanageable." Howard Zinn in *You Can't Be Neutral on a Moving Train*, a 2004 film by Deb Ellis and Denis Mueller. **151** b) A question asked by artist Marty Pottenger in Joan Braderman's 2009 film *The Heretics*. **152** l) He was a boy once. He was alone at the time of his arrest. Left his vehicle, makes nothing of his life. Where does music come from? **153** n) David Reed quoting Milton Resnik in Reed's essay "The Unsettling Mark," *Art in America* (September 2011), 90. // "A leaf is a leaf. But [making a small horizontal circle with his index finger] you gotta see all *around* the leaf. That's art." Joe Kocis (Thanks to Navesink Plumbing, Belford, N.J.). **154** v) Ben Massarella in *Made a Machine by Describing the Landscape*, a 2011 film by Solan Jensen & Joshua Marie Wilkinson. **155** x) The narrative style of the traditional ballad is described by Francis Barton Gummere as "alternate leaping and lingering" in *The Popular Ballad* (Nabu Press, 2010), originally published in 1907. **157** Amiri Baraka, "X." Reprinted by permission of SLL/Sterling Lord Literistic, Inc. Copyright by Amiri Baraka.

Although I was thinking in two-page spreads, at some point I realized that I wasn't actually (physically) making a book. I was making a big rectangular piece of temporary art.

about the author   visit kickingwind.com

169 I dream Frank Zappa stops by my house on the day he's going to die. He brings me a strange musical instrument he has invented, small and wide-necked with eight strings. He's selling them. We sit on the front steps for a couple of minutes. I already know about his death—I know about it from my waking life—so in the dream I know he only has six hours to live. Should I tell him? If he knew, wouldn't he want to spend his last day differently? Instead I buy an instrument and he continues on.

For a complete list of Ahsahta Press titles, visit
ahsahtapress.org

AHSAHTA PRESS

2013

JANET HOLMES, DIRECTOR

CHRISTOPHER CARUSO	RYAN HOLMAN
JODI CHILSON	MELISSA HUGHES, *intern*
KYLE CRAWFORD	TORIN JENSEN
CHARLES GABEL	ANNIE KNOWLES
JESSICA HAMBLETON, *intern*	STEPHA PETERS

JULIE STRAND